W9-BTN-192

INFLUENCING OTHERS

Successful Strategies For Persuasive Communication

William L. Nothstine

CRISP PUBLICATIONS, INC.
Los Altos, California

INFLUENCING OTHERS
Successful Strategies For
Persuasive Communication

William L. Nothstine

CREDITS
Editors: **Michael G. Crisp and Francine Lundy-Ruvolo**
Designer: **Carol Harris**
Typesetting: **Interface Studio**
Cover Design: **Carol Harris**
Artwork: **Ralph Mapson**

All rights reserved. No part of this book may be reproduced or transmitted in any form or by any means now known or to be invented, electronic or mechanical, including photocopying, recording, or by any information storage or retrieval system without written permission from the author or publisher, except for the brief inclusion of quotations in a review.

Copyright © 1989 by Crisp Publications, Inc.
Printed in the United States of America

Crisp books are distributed in Canada by Reid Publishing, Ltd., P.O. Box 7267, Oakville, Ontario, Canada L6J 6L6.

In Australia by Career Builders, P.O. Box 1051 Springwood, Brisbane, Queensland, Australia 4127.

And in New Zealand by Career Builders, P.O. Box 571, Manurewa, New Zealand.

Library of Congress Catalog Card Number 88-92734
Nothstine, William L.
Influencing Others
ISBN 0-931961-84-X

TO THE READER

The study of persuasion is a time-honored tradition, reaching back 2500 years to ancient Greece. Around that time, Plato was advising future leaders to learn the art of persuasion and to consider how the same words can have different effects on different listeners.

What the founders of the art emphasized, and what remains absolutely true today, is that effective persuasion involves not only good communication SKILLS, but also sound STRATEGY for using those skills in dealings with others. This book is mostly about strategy. For a greater emphasis on skills, you might also want to look at two other books from Crisp Publications: BETTER BUSINESS WRITING, and EFFECTIVE PRESENTATION SKILLS, which may be ordered using the form in the back of this book.

Forming effective strategy in influencing others through our speaking and writing depends upon us seeing that *virtually all of our important communication is persuasive*—to some extent.

The rules and guidelines in this book will often seem familiar to you—and they should! They describe not only the audiences we face as speakers and writers, but how we, ourselves, often react when others are trying to influence us. These principles have been proven, not only by ''common sense,'' but also by the work and study of experts in persuasion.

The effort you take to master and apply these principles in your own communication activities will be repaid many times over in professional success and personal satisfaction.

William L. Nothstine

ABOUT THIS BOOK

INFLUENCING OTHERS has a unique ''self-paced'' format that encourages a reader to become personally involved. Designed to be ''read with a pencil,'' this book contains an abundance of exercises that invite participation.

The objective of INFLUENCING OTHERS is to help people improve their ability to influence others through their communication, by providing basic communication strategies and allowing the readers to practice what they have learned.

INFLUENCING OTHERS and the other self-improvement books described at the back of this manual are valuable in several ways:

Individual Study. Because the book is self-instructional, all that is needed is a quiet place, time, and a pencil. Completing all the activities and exercises will provide practical steps for self-improvement.

Workshops and Seminars. This book is ideal as pre-assigned reading prior to a formal training session. With the basics in hand, more time can be spent on concept extensions and advanced applications. The book is also effective when used as a part of a workshop or seminar.

Remote Location Training. Copies can be sent to those not able to attend ''home office'' training sessions. INFLUENCING OTHERS also makes an excellent ''desk reference book.''

There are other possibilities that depend on the needs or objectives of the user. You are invited to find uses that will provide benefits for your program.

CONTENTS

SECTION I:
ABOUT PERSUASION

It's a familiar problem: Smith has a perfectly good idea, explains it clearly to Jones and Wilson, yet they don't follow Smith's advice. So good ideas are lost, good proposals lack support, or good decisions are not made. Why? You often wonder.

INFLUENCING OTHERS not only answers why, but also gives you the basic rules for anticipating and preventing such problems in your own communication.

ABOUT PERSUASION

We've all heard "myths" about persuasion—some are intended to make persuasion seem simpler that it really is, but most of them make persuasion much harder that it needs to be. The aim of this book is to expose these "myths" and give you practical advice for moving an audience to support your plans and proposals.

We will consider special strategies for: defusing truly hostile audiences, motivating undecided audiences, and bolstering sympathetic audiences. We'll look closely at various reasons for audience oppositon, and examine special techniques.

The result is a handbook of simple, proven rules to guide you when you attempt to influence an audience—large or small—through speaking or writing. If you have the basic oral and written communication skills, but still aren't as effective in your communication as you want to be, this is the book for you.

When do you need the guidelines contained in INFLUENCING OTHERS? Here are some examples of the way you influence people every day:

- Participating in employment and hiring interviews

- Influencing supervisors

- Working in problem-solving groups or committees

- Preparing reports for management

- Implementing new policies for subordinates

- Handling complaints from clients or customers

- Requesting special services from suppliers

ADD YOUR OWN:

- _____

- _____

Whether you are speaking to bosses, employees, partners, committee members, customers, business representatives, community members, or strangers, you need to be sensitive to your role as a persuasive communicator!

DEFINITIONS

The term ''persuasion'' will be central to this book, and it will be useful to clarify what it means.

PERSUASION refers to any attempt (successful, we hope!) to influence the actions or judgments of others by talking or writing to them. Many people use ''persuasion'' more broadly than this—to include use of physical force, or cases in which ''we persuade ourselves,'' for instance. In this book though, ''persuasion'' will always mean Person A speaking or writing seriously to influence Person B.

Also in this book we will use the word ''audience'' to refer to anyone or any group you are attempting to influence. This could be a large group of people in a formal speaking situation or a small group of people for whom you are composing a memo, or one other person you are talking to informally.

Many times, you might imagine that ''persuasion'' has nothing to do with our communication—but you are often wrong! One goal of this book is to make you more sensitive to the range of persuasion throughout your daily activities.

One last point: Don't be misled into thinking that ''persuasion'' means ''unfair manipulation'' or something equally negative. All communication is persuasive to some extent, as you will see. What makes ''persuasion'' a negative term is people who use its principles unethically. It's up to you to communicate responsibly and ethically.

''THINGS LOOK GREAT, DON'T THEY?''

SELF-ASSESSMENT

Before considering techniques for persuading different kinds of audiences, let's evaluate your attitudes as a communicator and a persuader. After you read each statement below, circle the number that best describes your agreement or disagreement. An explanation of the results immediately follows this self-test.

	AGREE		DISAGREE	

1. All you need to know about an audience is whether they are "for you" or "against you."   1   2   3   4   5

2. In order to communicate successfully all you need is a clear message. A clear, accurate explanation should convince an audience.   1   2   3   4   5

3. A friendly audience does not need persuasion.   1   2   3   4   5

4. The only way to be successful at persuasion is to take an audience from total disagreement to total agreement.   1   2   3   4   5

	AGREE		DISAGREE	

5. It's usually better not to persuade people; it's usually best to inform them.

    1   2   3   4   5

6. The best way to persuade an audience is to be totally logical, using statistics and documented facts.

    1   2   3   4   5

7. If you've explained your position to your audience, clearly, logically and accurately, they will be persuaded.

    1   2   3   4   5

8. If something strikes me as persuasive, it probably will be persuasive for the next person, too.

    1   2   3   4   5

9. If all people had access to the same facts, persuasion wouldn't be needed.

    1   2   3   4   5

Total score: _____

SEE NEXT PAGE
FOR SCORING RESULTS

SCORING SUMMARY

The statements on the previous two pages are ''myths'' about persuasion. Although some of them may contain a grain of truth, they are risky guides for your communication and persuasion. This book will look at the ''realities'' of persuasion, and show how they compare with these ''myths.''

If your total score was between 35 and 45, you are probably already successful in most of your communication, although some problems may arise from time to time. You have the right attitude about persuasion and can use this book to refine your strategies for specific situations.

If your total score was between 28 and 34, this book can show you how to use the skills you already have to make better choices as a persuader.

If your total was between 22 and 28, this book should help you make a noticeable improvement in your effectiveness as a persuader.

If your total was below 22, this book has a great deal of help to offer you. It's going to be challenging at times—re-thinking some of your basic assumptions—but you can do it, and the rewards will be more than worth the work!

At the conclusion of the book we'll review these ''myths'' again, giving you a chance to see your progress.

THE DIFFERENCE BETWEEN SKILLS AND STRATEGIES

1. Think about the ways in which effective communication is like a game. Assume that people are involved, and that they will follow the basic rules of the game or situation, even though they are competing.

2. Both in games and in communication we must master the fundamental skills and abilities. In football, we would have to learn passing, catching, blocking, and tackling; in golf, we would have to learn the correct stance, grip, and swing for various clubs. In communication, the fundamentals include organizing, using evidence and visual aids, learning effective posture and gestures, and so on.

3. Perhaps most important for success—in both games and communication is that we have to think in terms of the larger picture in order to use the appropriate strategy in a given situation. In football, we need to know when it's better to advance the ball ourselves, and when it's better to give it to a teammate. In golf, we need to know when to "play safe" and when to take a risky shot. In communication, we need to know which abilities to use in a particular situation.

For example, all communicators know that it's important to establish credibility as a speaker or writer—but when do we do that by showing how we're *like* our audience, and when should we do that by showing how *unlike* our audience we are? That's strategy!

Similarly, all good communicators know that having support for our claims is important—but when should we use statistics, when should we use the testimony of experts, and when should we use examples, case studies, or anecdotes? That's strategy!

Experience, teaching, or self-improvement study, give you important opportunities to learn important communication skills. This book will teach you larger organizing patterns—*strategies*—that will guide you to use your communication skills more effectively and persuasively in different situations and with different audiences.

GOAL SETTING

In the rest of this book, we're going to apply the basic skills of communication to guidelines for different kinds of persuasive situations and audiences. Based on the results of the preceding self-test, what goals do you want to achieve in using this book?

I intend to:

☐ work to substitute proven guidelines of persuasive strategy for any myths about persuasion I may have.

☐ improve my ability to read contextual clues so that I may anticipate resistance from a given audience.

☐ improve my ability to analyze communication situations to determine the general kind of strategy needed.

☐ improve my ability to apply my communication skills to deflect or defuse resistance to persuasion that might prevent my success.

_____

Your Name   Date

SECTION II: UNDERSTANDING THE WHY'S AND WHENS OF PERSUASION

TRUST ME. IT'LL BE GREAT! TERRIFIC! YOU'LL SEE... IT'LL WORK!

The first step in being a more effective persuader is being able to anticipate *why* and *when* you need to persuade. If other people are making the decisions you want, or taking the actions you believe are appropriate, then you might not need to influence them through persuasion. Unfortunately, this is not often the case!

EXAMPLES OF PERSUASION

Many times you will have to act as a persuader, speaking and/or writing to influence the judgments of others. For example, you may need to:

Cope with the members of another division at work who are promoting a proposal that competes with one you are trying to get approved; or

''Smooth the feathers'' of employees who think your new billing procedures will give them less control over purchasing; or

Convince your boss that bonuses for the department will save him or her money through increased productivity and lower turnover; or

Show a personnel manager why your application, even though it doesn't fit the ''typical'' mold, nevertheless qualifies you for the position you want.

Add Your Own:

_____

_____

_____

_____

NINE COMMUNICATION MYTHS

Throughout the balance of this book you will be introduced to nine myths dealing with communication. By becoming aware of what they are and how to react to each, you will learn the basics of positive influence. Several exercises and activities will allow you to practice what you have learned about each myth.

COMMUNICATION MYTH #1

COMMUNICATION MYTH #1: All you need to know about an audience is whether they are ''for you'' or ''against you.''

AMOUNT OF RESISTANCE VERSUS THE SOURCE OF RESISTANCE

Remember the mention of ''communication myths'' from Section I? This is a good time to begin correcting them. Let's start with one of the most important:

It is important to remember that *what* people feel is different from *why* they feel it!

To select an effective persuasive strategy, you must first determine the amount of resistance—you might think of this as the distance between where the audience is now and where you want them to be. Then, you need to determine the sources of resistance—the ''why's'' that explain how your audience came to hold judgments different from yours.

In this section, you are going to look closely at different strategies based upon the amount of resistance; in SECTION III you will examine the sources of resistance.

Let us begin by cataloguing the general types of audiences you might have to influence and the amount of resistance you might face.

THERE ARE BETTER METHODS OF PERSUASION

DETERMINING THE TYPE OF AUDIENCE

In general, you, the communicator, will face seven types of audiences. They are listed below. The audiences you encounter will be:

1. **OPENLY OR ACTIVELY UNFRIENDLY.** This audience is your greatest challenge. These people oppose your position so strongly that they are willing to work actively against you—perhaps by speaking out in opposition to you, or rallying support against you and your ideas.

2. **UNFRIENDLY.** This audience disagrees with your position, but not necessarily to the point of taking counter-action. For example, an audience may not vote for your proposal even though they may not actively campaign against it.

3. **NEUTRAL.** A neutral audience understands your position but isn't particularly for or against you. Perhaps these people feel that the outcome wouldn't affect them either way, so they have no strong preference for one side or another.

4. **UNDECIDED.** This audience understands your position, but feels torn between reasons to support you and reasons not to support you. An Undecided audience is not neutral; people here do care about the issue involved, but they don't yet see a clear reason to decide one way or the other.

5. **UNINFORMED.** If the audience is uninformed it has no solid opinion one way or the other about your position because these people are unfamiliar with it and the issues behind it. An UNINFORMED audience is not the same as a NEUTRAL audience or an UNDECIDED audience—the two latter audiences still understand your position—but an UNINFORMED audience doesn't.

6. **SUPPORTIVE.** You like this audience. It understands your position and feels positively inclined toward it, although not necessarily to the point of taking action to help you, yet.

or

7. **OPENLY OR ACTIVELY SUPPORTIVE.** You love this audience. Not only does it agree with your position, but it is willing (perhaps already has begun) to work actively in support of your position or idea.

Many people are surprised to think about SEVEN different audience types! It's a myth to imagine that all audiences are alike. The reality is that audiences offer different amounts of support or resistance. What seems "clear" (or persuasive) to one audience may have a totally different effect on another. That leads us to the second myth we need to dispel.

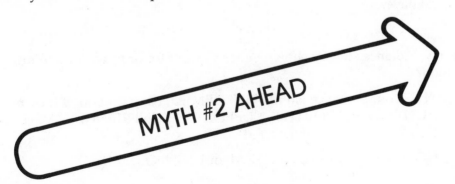

MYTH #2 AHEAD

COMMUNICATION MYTH #2

COMMUNICATION MYTH #2: In order to communicate successfully all you need is a clear message.

The reality is that you must analyze your audience to find out how SUPPORTIVE or UNFRIENDLY it is. How do you find out which kind of audience you have? Do your homework!

While you're planning your message, find out as much about your prospective audience as you can. If possible, talk to members of the audience, and talk to others who have dealt with them. Think about the things you may have already heard them say or do that would give you some clue about their attitudes. Imagine how you would feel and act if you were in their position. Try to find out what they already know (or think they know!) about you and your ideas.

WHAT KIND OF AUDIENCE DO YOU HAVE?

As a guide to determining the kind of audience you're going to face, review the following questions, and match the answers to the categories from pages 12 and 13.

1. Does my audience know already anything about what I have to say to them?

_____ NO. You have an UNINFORMED audience and should choose your strategies accordingly.

_____ YES. Go on to questions 2 and 3 to find out what kind of audience you do have.

2. Has my audience already shown either support for or opposition to my position?

_____ YES. Your audience isn't UNINFORMED. Now find out if they're ACTIVELY SUPPORTIVE, SUPPORTIVE, UNFRIENDLY, ACTIVELY UNFRIENDLY, or UNDECIDED.

_____ NO. Is your audience NEUTRAL or UNINFORMED?

COMMUNICATION MYTH #2
(Continued)

3. Has my audience ever done anything that would categorize it as an ACTIVE audience—either ACTIVELY UNFRIENDLY or ACTIVELY SUPPORTIVE?

____ YES. Choose your strategies accordingly.

____ NO. Determine if it is UNDECIDED or NEUTRAL.

***PERSUADING EFFECTIVELY MEANS
DOING YOUR HOMEWORK***

COMMUNICATION MYTH #3

COMMUNICATION MYTH #3: Only unfriendly audiences require persuasive communication—friendly ones are already on your side.

It is important to form the right expectations as a persuader, and the point at which you determine the amount of resistance in your audience is a good time to work on those expectations.

Why are SUPPORTIVE and ACTIVELY SUPPORTIVE audiences included here, you ask? If they already agree, why do we need to persuade them? The answer is simple, but—once again—it often separates the successful persuaders from the less successful ones!

First, you may need to motivate SUPPORTIVE audiences to action—that's persuasion.

Second, you may need to guide ACTIVELY SUPPORTIVE audiences to the RIGHT KIND OF ACTION—that's persuasion.

Finally, you may need to keep an ACTIVELY SUPPORTIVE audience from losing interest, encouraging them to stay active—that's persuasion, too!

MOVE YOUR AUDIENCE IN THE RIGHT DIRECTION

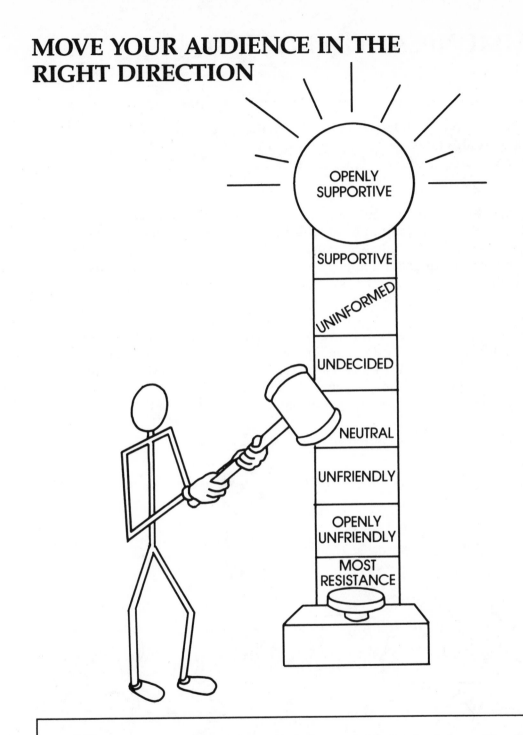

Remember: Any movement from the bottom of this list (openly unfriendly) toward the top (openly supportive) is persuasion!

For example, if an ACTIVELY UNFRIENDLY audience can be made into an UNFRIENDLY audience—still hostile, but not ACTIVELY working against you—that's persuasion, and you're better off than you were before!

COMMUNICATION MYTH #4

COMMUNICATION MYTH #4: Persuasion means converting an unfriendly audience into a supportive audience.

Many people think "persuasion" only means making an UNFRIENDLY audience into a SUPPORTIVE one, but in reality this is rare. It's often unrealistic to expect dramatic change from an audience, especially if you don't have much time to work with them. Frequently, you will have the chance to make only limited change with an audience; don't miss the chance by having the wrong expectations.

Anything that defuses an ACTIVELY UNFRIENDLY audience, or moves an UNFRIENDLY audience to indecision, or motivates a SUPPORTIVE audience to action, or bolsters an ACTIVELY SUPPORTIVE audience is working to your advantage. For any audience, ask yourself, "How much change am I likely to get from these people?" Then set your sights on getting every bit of that, if you can!

"MY GOAL TODAY IS TO MOVE YOU FROM BEING ACTIVELY UNFRIENDLY TO SIMPLY UNFRIENDLY"

COMMUNICATION MYTH #5

COMMUNICATION MYTH #5: ''Persuading'' and ''informing'' are two different things.

There's a difference between audiences that are NEUTRAL, UNDECIDED, and UNINFORMED! Many people ignore the difference, but effective communicators know the need to keep them separate. Note this very important fact:

''Informative'' speaking or writing is really a kind of PERSUASIVE communication—it's persuasive communication directed to an audience whose disagreement with you rests on the fact that they don't have much information—an UNINFORMED audience.

''MY TWO OBJECTIVES TODAY ARE TO INFORM YOU AND TO PERSUADE YOU''

A PRACTICE SESSION

IDENTIFYING TYPES OF AUDIENCES

''Friend or foe?'' Before we go any further, take a few moments to test your ability to identify examples of the different audience types we've looked at above.

Imagine that the information provided below is what you've learned about the audience you'll be facing. Is the audience likely to be (1) ACTIVELY UNFRIENDLY, (2) UNFRIENDLY, (3) NEUTRAL, (4) UNDECIDED, (5) UNINFORMED, (6) SUPPORTIVE, or (7) ACTIVELY SUPPORTIVE?

(Write in the number you feel best describes the situation and compare your answer with that of the author on page 22):

☐ **1.** As secretary of your local union, you're going to speak to the members about a change in the normal procedures for voting in the upcoming election. Instead of allowing each member to vote for two candidates, then having a ''run-off'' among the top three, each member will vote for only one candidate and the person with the most votes will be elected. The members who vote tend to be those who have belonged to the union the longest; newer members don't tend to vote as much.

☐ **2.** Your neighborhood has had a series of break-ins and acts of vandalism and you've called a meeting of residents to explore ways to react as a community. All agree that something needs to be done: some want to organize neighborhood watches, some want to petition the city council for better police protection and others have different suggestions.

IDENTIFYING SUPPORTING AND UNFRIENDLY AUDIENCES (Continued)

☐ **3.** Your manufacturing plant, under newly-passed ''right to know'' laws, is going to have to notify the community of any hazardous chemicals used in production. Your plant has been in the community for thirty years, using chemicals and processes that have remained largely unchanged during that time. Your company has no reason to believe that the chemicals used in your manufacturing pose any unusual danger to the community. Other companies in your industry have faced hostility when their local communities learned of the presence of hazardous chemicals in their area.

☐ **4.** Your company's customer service staff takes pride in meeting customer needs. In order to incorporate new office equipment to help them do their jobs better, the staff will have to spend less time with each customer. The staff supports acquiring the new equipment, but is unhappy about the reduction in customer contact.

''REMEMBER THE GOOD OLD DAYS WHEN WE USED TO MEET WITH CUSTOMERS?''

AUTHOR RESPONSES: (Compare Your Answers)

1. **UNINFORMED.** Unless you knew of some reason why the members would resist the change, the description suggests the audience will be UNINFORMED—the main problem is they simply don't know about the change in procedures yet. (The newer members are probably NEUTRAL, since they're unlikely to view the change as affecting them much.)

2. **ACTIVELY SUPPORTIVE.** From the description, it sounds—at least for now—like an ACTIVELY SUPPORTIVE audience. They're all concerned, they've all shown at least enough commitment to come to the meeting. You'll need to discover ways to keep them motivated. As you begin to discuss specific ways to address the problem you can expect disagreements and differences of opinion to emerge, thus producing smaller sub-audiences—some SUPPORTIVE, some UNFRIENDLY, and so on.

3. **UNINFORMED.** This description suggests that your audience may be UNINFORMED since they probably don't know much about your manufacturing processes or the chemicals involved. However, don't be surprised if the dominant reaction from the community ranges from UNFRIENDLY to ACTIVELY UNFRIENDLY when they learn that a plant in their community uses hazardous chemicals.

4. **UNDECIDED.** This audience sounds UNDECIDED. They understand the choices, but they face a conflict in values—improving working conditions for themselves versus spending more time with customers. Remember: people are people. They care about, want, or believe in many different things. Sometimes, these different wants and beliefs come into conflict, leaving them UNDECIDED.

Of course, in some of these cases, it's difficult (and misleading) to draw sharp, absolute lines—to say ''this audience is purely SUPPORTIVE or definitely NEUTRAL.'' Categories should not be treated as ''either-or,'' or ''black-or-white'' divisions. The more information you can obtain about your audience in advance, the more confidence you will have in your ''reading'' of them.

GENERAL STRATEGIES BASED ON DEGREE OF RESISTANCE OR SUPPORT

In SECTION III you will look at specialized strategies for dealing with *why* certain audiences are hostile or undecided, but for now you will consider the general strategies for each type of audience—from ACTIVELY UNFRIENDLY to ACTIVELY SUPPORTIVE.

ACTIVELY UNFRIENDLY AUDIENCE STRATEGIES:

The most important thing is to "de-ACTIVE-ate" them! Even if they remain UNFRIENDLY, nothing matters as much as getting them to stop actively working against you!

In general, work to build a positive relationship with an ACTIVELY UNFRIENDLY audience.

The following techniques are for ACTIVELY UNFRIENDLY audiences. When an opportunity comes up, I plan to: (Check those you intend to use)

☐ Stress areas of agreement as much as possible before getting into areas of disagreement with my audience.

☐ "Break the ice" with some humor or a friendly story.

☐ If possible, meet with my audience more than once before confronting them on areas of disagreement. Let them find out I'm a "real human being."

☐ Tell them that my position is not the only solution or viewpoint. Respect their feelings and integrity, while still working to promote my position.

☐ Work with experts and authorities that the group will respect, even if these are not my first choice. (There are two reasons for this: first, they're not interested in why you're convinced; they want to know why they should be—by telling them in terms they'll understand will help my case. Second, being able to talk about their concerns will show them, I respect their point of view, and that I've "done my homework."

GENERAL STRATEGIES (Continued)

UNFRIENDLY AUDIENCE STRATEGIES

Sometimes UNFRIENDLY audiences can become SUPPORTIVE audiences. In many cases, though, an UNFRIENDLY audience can only be moved to being UNDECIDED—no longer totally opposing you, but not yet giving full support, either. Remember: either way, you're better off than you were before!

In general, show UNFRIENDLY audiences that you are being careful, fair, and logical.

The following techniques are for UNFRIENDLY audiences. Look for opportunities to use them. I plan to:

☐ Avoid making any important statements without the evidence to support them. I will be able to show where all my information came from.

☐ Be clear about where I disagree with the audience. I won't overdo it because I want to build as much rapport and common ground as possible before expressing my disagreement.

☐ Ask for a little and get it, rather than to ask for a lot and be turned down. I will try to secure a limited, partial commitment to get them used to the idea of agreeing on smaller issues. Then they'll be more inclined to help me later with something more important.

☐ Avoid simply convincing myself that I'm being logical. I realize that I must convince the audience, too! I will lay out my reasoning as clearly and as carefully as possible from my basic assumptions to my final conclusions.

☐ Avoid conclusions that don't come strictly from my premises. When I'm in doubt, I'll draw more modest conclusions, rather than risk getting caught exaggerating.

☐ Demonstrate my understanding of other sides of the issue as well as my own. I'll be alert for ways to stress ''win-win'' outcomes rather than ''win-lose'' outcomes.

☐ Stress areas of agreement and common ground before introducing areas of disagreement or controversy.

☐ Use statistics or any numerical information accurately and fairly and tell my audience where any numbers or data came from.

☐ Only use experts and authorities that the audience will recognize and respect.

☐ Only use examples (case studies, stories, or narratives), that are actual, ''real-life'' examples, not fictional ones. I will select examples that my audience will find representative and I will draw clear conclusions from these examples.

ACTIVE UNFRIENDLY AUDIENCES CAN BE FRIGHTENING IF YOU ARE NOT PREPARED.

GENERAL STRATEGIES (Continued)

NEUTRAL AUDIENCE STRATEGIES

NEUTRAL audiences neither support nor oppose you. They understand the issue but feel no connection to it.

> In general, associate your issue with a NEUTRAL audience's feelings, values and concerns, and attempt to move them to a position of support.

The following techniques are for NEUTRAL audiences when an opportunity comes I intend to: (Check those you plan to use)

☐ Stress the connection between my proposal or position and the interest of my audience.

☐ Draw attention to my position even if it means downplaying or ignoring opposing points of view.

☐ Avoid complex arguments by focusing on simple and vivid claims that I restate in many different forms.

☐ Stress not only mutual benefits, but also mutual losses if my ideas aren't accepted. I'll be alert for "common enemies" I might share with my audience.

☐ Describe vivid pictures of how much better things will be if they support me. I can help them visualize the improvements.

☐ Draw heavily on concrete examples, with familiar situations, characters, or events.

COMMUNICATION MYTH #6

COMMUNICATION MYTH #6: It's always best to rely on statistics to influence people.

Many people believe that the only way to convince people is with statistics or other numerical information. As you've seen already, and will see again, some situations and some audiences don't call for statistics. Most that do call for numerical information will usually also require that you strengthen those dry, impersonal numbers with something ''real'' such as concrete examples, hypothetical scenarios, case studies, testimony of experts or witnesses, and so on.

''SO YOU CAN NOW CLEARLY SEE THAT APPLES ARE GOOD FOR YOU''

GENERAL STRATEGIES (Continued)

UNDECIDED AUDIENCE STRATEGIES

UNDECIDED audiences are ''hanging'' between supporting you and not supporting you.

> In general, work to ''Tip the Scales''—even slightly—in your favor with an undecided audience, moving them to become supportive (or even actively supportive!)

The following techniques are for UNDECIDED audiences. When I have the opportunity I plan to:

☐ Focus attention on my side of the issue. I will not misrepresent the other side, but I won't worry as much about a ''balanced'' presentation as I might with an UNFRIENDLY audience.

☐ Support my case with examples and expert testimony. I will not rely exclusively on statistics. If I do use statistics, I'll make sure that they are simple and relevant. I will intermix them with examples (preferably real ones) that will add clarity and force.

☐ Quote from experts the audience knows and respects. I will use quotes that are vivid, forceful, and colorful.

☐ Use examples to dramatize and ''personalize'' my case. I want to make my audience ''feel'' as much as ''think.''

☐ Be more aggressive in drawing my conclusions than I might with a HOSTILE audience. I'll be honest, but won't be afraid to exaggerate my conclusions to reinforce my case.

☐ Look for ways to break my proposal into smaller action items my audience can accept. I know that once an audience has taken even a small step in my direction, it will be easier to move them more, later.

☐ Whenever possible, follow up with my audience, since—even if I convince them—I know an UNDECIDED audience may reverse its position if it is not reinforced.

UNINFORMED AUDIENCE STRATEGIES

Remember that influencing UNINFORMED audiences is still persuasion—it's still using speaking or writing to influence their judgments. (We never really try to "inform" people without assuming or hoping that they'll act or feel differently based on the new information, do we?)

In general, the strategy for persuading uninformed audiences is to downplay the fact that any persuasion is going on!

The following techniques are for an UNINFORMED audience. When I see the opportunity I plan to:

☐ Stress my credibility—especially any special expertise, experience, or training I have.

☐ Discuss my side of the issue without paying attention to the others.

☐ Work especially hard to develop a clear structure. This can best be accomplished through a careful and clear organization. I will preview each point that I make, and after each point, I will summarize and remind the audience of its connection to the main issue.

☐ Not expect too much at once. With limited goals, I will avoid the temptation to "bury" my audience in information.

☐ Encourage my audience to learn. I will invite questions and requests for clarification.

☐ Alternate between statistical (numerical) support and concrete examples that illustrate my point.

☐ Make my message lively and interesting in order to keep their attention.

GENERAL STRATEGIES (Continued)

SUPPORTIVE AUDIENCE STRATEGIES

SUPPORTIVE audiences provide a different challenge than the kinds discussed so far. With SUPPORTIVE audiences your goal is to strengthen and reinforce, encouraging them and even motivating them to become ACTIVELY SUPPORTIVE.

> In general, the strategy for supportive audiences is to engage their enthusiasm and set clear behavioral goals.

The following techniques are for SUPPORTIVE audiences. When I see an opportunity, I will:

☐ Ask for clear action. Make sure my audience knows what needs to be done and what their individual parts are.

☐ Try to get my audience to act *as soon as possible.*

☐ Reinforce their commitment with vivid testimonials and examples of the "good results" others have gotten from this approach.

☐ Use examples and testimony to intensify the commitment of the audience, not to "prove" my position. For a supportive audience it's already proven!

☐ Stress "group identity," encouraging them to feel a "belonging" to each other and the cause.

☐ Prepare the audience for possible encounters with others who may be HOSTILE to the topic. I will teach them what to expect from "unbelievers" and show them how to defend their position.

ACTIVELY SUPPORTIVE AUDIENCE STRATEGIES

This is your "dream" audience, but don't take them for granted. Don't let them become inactive.

The most important objective with an ACTIVELY SUPPORTIVE audience is to keep them active!

The following techniques are for ACTIVELY SUPPORTIVE audiences. When I see an opportunity I plan to:

☐ Invite audience members to encourage one another, discussing their successes or positive feelings about my ideas.

☐ Look for ways to stress "unfinished work," or a "common enemy" still to be overcome.

☐ As the audience seems close to reaching preset goals, I will try to get them to commit to new but related goals.

☐ If the audience tends to be moderately active, but not holding extreme views, I will keep motivating them to action. If the audience tends to be more militant or aggressive, and inclined to extreme views or courses of action, I will work to achieve discipline among them.

KEEP SUPPORTIVE AUDIENCES ENTHUSED!

A WORD ABOUT MIXED AUDIENCES

Mixed audiences may contain some members who are UNFRIENDLY, some who are NEUTRAL, or perhaps some who are UNINFORMED or even SUPPORTIVE. Very few audiences are purely NEUTRAL, or purely SUPPORTIVE, and so on. It is often not difficult to identify a "pure" audience (composed almost completely of one of the seven types we've discussed): the situation itself will often screen certain types of audiences out. For example, a political rally will provide an audience that is mostly ACTIVELY SUPPORTIVE, since they've demonstrated their active commitment by attending in the first place.

HERE ARE SOME IMPORTANT GUIDELINES FOR MIXED AUDIENCES:

First, ask yourself: which parts of the audience do you *really need* to influence? Are some groups numerically larger than the others? Do some groups have more power to help (or hinder) you than others? If so, focus your efforts more on these sections of your audience.

For example, most politicians pay special attention, in their campaign speeches, advertisements, and fliers, to issues of interest to large blocks of voters, and to those citizens who vote regularly. This is *not* because infrequent voters are unimportant, or because the concerns of numerically-small groups are unimportant—it's because politicians, as persuaders, need large groups of voters who can be counted on to vote. Success among other groups may be a moral victory, but won't contribute to the reason for campaigning in the first place—election!

2

Second, where it's possible, try to address different parts of your audience with different parts of your message. Look for ways to influence each group in your direction, even if that means having different incentives at different points in your message.

For example, take a tip from advertisers, who deal with large, diverse audiences. Remember those advertisements for snack food that promise good taste to the kids, while assuring Mom that the treats are still healthy and nutritious? A commercial that can appeal to both audiences will probably be successful.

3

Third, never attempt to be "all things to all people." Trying to satisfy several different sub-audiences, with competing agendas, may "turn off" all of your audience.

Think about politicians again. One sure way to discredit a political candidate is to show that he or she is "saying different things to different groups." A candidate who tells farmers today that he supports farm subsidies, and tomorrow tells suburbanites he supports lower food prices, may rightly be seen as untrustworthy in the eyes of BOTH groups. A candidate who tells blue collar workers Monday that she supports the union workers, and on Tuesday tells managers and owners that she supports big business, may end up an enemy on BOTH sides.

REVIEW: SELECTING STRATEGIES
FOR DIFFERENT AUDIENCES

Before you move to the next section of the book, take a few moments to review
what you've learned in this section by responding to the four case studies that
follow. Remember these questions: *How much* resistance or support should I
expect? And *what strategies* should I use for this kind of audience?

Compare your answers to those of the author on page 38.

CASE #1: In a scheduled salary review meeting with your boss, you want to
ask for a raise. You know that your ratings for this review period have been
good, but you also know that the money for raises is scarce this year. Two
other people with roughly similar evaluations have been turned down for a
raise. Because of timing of your transfer into this division, you missed one
scheduled raise already. Your supervisor and you have always been on a
friendly basis.

---

1. What kind of audience will you face (e.g., UNFRIENDLY, NEUTRAL, etc.)?

_____

2. What can you reasonably expect to accomplish in this situation?

_____

_____

3. Based on the recommended strategies for such an audience, list at least **three**
specific things you might say or do to influence your audience. (For example,
what might you say to build common ground, or to enhance your credibility?
What statistics, examples, or testimony might you use?)

_____

_____

_____

_____

_____

REVIEW (Continued)

CASE #2: You have been asked to prepare a report for your boss on the advisability of purchasing a new computer system for your department. You know that your boss is not eager to spend the money, but you also know that the boss doesn't understand the new system, how it works, or what it could do. Based on your research, you've become convinced that the purchase of the new computer system would be a great benefit to your department.

---

1. What kind of audience will you face (e.g., UNFRIENDLY, NEUTRAL, etc.)?

   _____

2. What can you reasonably expect to accomplish in this situation?

   _____

   _____

3. Based on the recommended strategies for such an audience, list at least **three** specific things you might say or do to influence your audience. (For example, what might you say to build common ground, or to enhance your credibility? What statistics, examples, or testimony might you use?)

   _____

   _____

   _____

   _____

   _____

   _____

REVIEW (Continued)

CASE #3: You are attending a meeting of the parent-teachers organization at your local school. The teachers have asked for raises in their contract for next year—their first raise in two years. Most of those present at this meeting to discuss the proposed contract are opposed to the raise, since it will raise local taxes. You believe that the teachers deserve the raise, and that better salaries will attract better teachers to the school. When discussion is invited, you rise to speak briefly in favor of the new contract.

---

1. What kind of audience will you face (e.g., UNFRIENDLY, NEUTRAL, etc.)?

   _____

2. What can you reasonably expect to accomplish in this situation?

   _____

   _____

3. Based on the recommended strategies for such an audience, list at least **three** specific things you might say or do to influence your audience. (For example, what might you say to build common ground, or to enhance your credibility? What statistics, examples, or testimony might you use?)

   _____

   _____

   _____

   _____

   _____

   _____

REVIEW (Continued)

> **CASE #4:** Now, think about a ''real'' situation you are going to face—at work, at school, in some group or organization you belong to—where you'd like to influence your audience to support (or stop hindering) your ideas or plans. Ask yourself the very same questions:

1. What kind of audience will you face (e.g., UNFRIENDLY, NEUTRAL, etc.)?

   _____

2. What can you reasonably expect to accomplish in this situation?

   _____

   _____

3. Based on the recommended strategies for such an audience, list at least **three** specific things you might say or do to influence your audience. (For example, what might you say to build common ground, or to enhance your credibility? What statistics, examples, or testimony might you use?)

   _____

   _____

   _____

   _____

   _____

   _____

AUTHOR'S RESPONSES TO THE CASE STUDIES

Your list of specific things to say or do for each case will probably be different from the examples offered below. But, these examples employ the same strategies that you used in preparing your answers, and they're a good way to tell if you're on the right track!

CASE #1:

1. **Audience Type.**
   Your boss sounds UNDECIDED: caught between giving you the raise you want and saving scarce funds. The problem is not an audience who is UNFRIENDLY, NEUTRAL, OR UNINFORMED—instead it's a sympathetic audience who's caught between two important responsibilities.

2. **Reasonable Expectation.**
   Don't give up on the raise—try to convince the boss. BUT look for ways "to take the sting out of it" for your boss: perhaps settling for a somewhat lower figure at this time than you'd originally planned? (Remember that once you get an audience to support you, it's easier to get them to support you again later.) Or perhaps trading a straight raise for something less financially painful for the boss, like some extra vacation time?

3. **Tactics.**
   Based on the guidelines presented in this chapter, some potentially effective tactics are:

   - Keep the conversation away from topics that don't work in your favor, like the boss' money problems and the other employees who didn't get raises.

   - Stress the "fairness" issue—you're overdue for a raise. Give the boss the chance to feel good about giving you the raise.

   - Stress particular, concrete successes you've had in the department, especially those the boss has seen or been a part of. Don't count on the dry number ratings on your evaluation form—you're a real person!

AUTHOR RESPONSES (Continued)

CASE #2:

1. **Audience Type.**
   Here, your boss sounds UNINFORMED, although perhaps slightly UNFRIENDLY, depending on how serious a problem the cost of the new equipment might be. The problem seems to be less that the boss opposes the idea, than that he simply doesn't know much about it, yet.

2. **Reasonable Expectation.**
   Assuming that the system has to be bought in its entirety or not at all (it can't be purchased a little at a time), it probably makes sense to proceed CAUTIOUSLY toward asking for the authorization to purchase.

3. **Tactics.**
   Based on the guidelines presented in this chapter, some potentially effective tactics are:

   - Don't present yourself as asking the boss to decide on the purchase of the new system; present yourself as simply educating him about a new system and its advantages.

   - Don't confuse or overwhelm your boss with a lot of new information presented all at once. Begin with the most simple and obvious features and advantages, then move gradually into the more subtle and detailed information.

   - If possible, don't just *tell* about the system—*show* it. Let the boss work with the equipment, visualize it in the office, become familiar with it.

   - If you think the audience is significantly UNFRIENDLY—i.e., the expense is a serious obstacle—then consider scheduling more than one meeting about the new system. In the first meetings the issue of purchase should not even be brought up. Only after more interest has been generated should the troublesome point of money be mentioned.

AUTHOR RESPONSES (Continued)

CASE #3:

1. **Audience Type.**
This audience may be mixed, but the description indicates that the largest and most important group in the audience is UNFRIENDLY—probably ACTIVELY UNFRIENDLY, since they're committed enough to come to this meeting to speak out against giving the teachers a raise.

2. **Reasonable Expectation.**
It's unrealistic to expect to convert this audience to a FRIENDLY one—the issue is too important and you have too little time right now. Your best chance is to defuse their hostility as much as you can. They may still not agree with you when you finish, but perhaps they won't work actively against the new contract—and maybe further persuasion, a little later, can soften their position still more.

3. **Tactics.**
Based on the guidelines presented in this chapter, some potentially effective tactics are:

- Stress areas of agreement—you're a taxpayer, too; everyone wants the best education possible for the children of the community; you're a member of this community and take pride in it; and so on.

- Make it clear that you don't think it's foolish or unreasonable to want to keep local taxes down, but that good reasons exist for raising salaries, too.

- When you refer to authorities or experts, avoid experts from the teachers' side; try to find your support from the words and actions of the administration or the members of the audience. This audience would EXPECT the teachers to want a raise, and would probably rationalize away arguments built on what the teachers have said. Using the school board's words to support your position, on the other hand, would be a lot harder for this audience to ignore!

- If you use facts or figures, be sure that they are accurate. Listen to yourself carefully as you speak to make sure you don't mistakenly give incorrect information.

AUTHOR RESPONSES (Continued)

CASE #4:

Here's your chance to REALLY test yourself in your own work or other activities!

Remember: *First,* use whatever information about the audience and the situation you can find to determine how much resistance or support you can expect to encounter. *Next,* decide how much success you can reasonably expect to have with this audience, given what you know about them. *Finally,* as you prepare to communicate with them—speaking or writing—use the guidelines in this section, in addition to your basic speaking and writing skills, to form a strategy designed to help you reach your goal with this audience!

WHAT'S NEXT?

In Section III, we'll shift focus slightly.

Now that we've looked at the degree of resistance to expect in communicating successfully with a particular audience, it's time to consider the *reasons why* an audience might hold a particular position or point of view.

If you can determine *why* an audience believes, feels, or acts as it does, you can adopt strategies to increase your chances of influencing them successfully.

SECTION III: SOURCES OF RESISTANCE TO PERSUASION

In Section II we examined the different degrees to which an audience can support or disagree with you. We also looked at communication strategies appropriate to each type of audience. But that's only half of what needs to be done. In addition to knowing what an audience feels about your plan, proposal, etc., it's important to understand why the audience feels the way they do. Section III will examine reasons for resistance and identify specific strategies to deal with them.

THE CRITICAL QUESTION TO ASK YOURSELF

To understand why your audience feels a certain way, it is important to ask yourself the following question:

> "Okay, I accept that my audience (or most of them) are UNDECIDED (or UNFRIENDLY, or whichever category you identify)—but *why* do they feel this way?"

Or, put another way:

> "If my idea, plan, or point of view is as good as I believe, *why* isn't my audience already on my side? What's keeping them from agreeing with me?"

Think about when others have tried to influence you. Whether you were—FRIENDLY, or NEUTRAL, or ACTIVELY UNFRIENDLY—you always had a reason for your feelings. It might have been your values that formed your position, or it might have been information on the subject you had access to, or it might have been how you felt about the person who was trying to influence you—but there was always a reason.

In this Section, we will examine the most common reasons for resistance, and in Section IV we'll look at specific strategies for attempting to overcome these sources of resistance. We'll proceed just like we did in Sections I and II—first identifying where we stand with our audience, and then devising strategies for influencing that audience successfully.

POSSIBLE SOURCES OF RESISTANCE

In general, the most common reasons *why* an audience initially resists the plan, ideas, or point of view you support will include:

---

1. CONFLICTING VALUES, ATTITUDES, OR LOYALTIES.

2. APATHY OR SKEPTICISM.

3. A NEGATIVE IMAGE OF YOU AS A COMMUNICATOR.

Strategies for dealing with the first two reasons were mentioned in Section II:

Audiences with conflicting values, attitudes or beliefs are UNDECIDED.

Audiences who are apathetic or skeptical are NEUTRAL.

The third reason for resistance, when your image as a communicator is negative, is different from the other two, because it doesn't simply involve the audience; *it involves you!* Your credibility, the image that the audience has of you, is the most important single factor in determining your success at influencing others.

Because your credibility is so important, it will be considered in more detail on the next page.

WHAT IS YOUR IMAGE?

A NEGATIVE IMAGE COMPROMISES YOUR CREDIBILITY

This source of resistance is most important to understand and correct. We have all at times resisted others who have tried to influence us simply because of who they were.

From a purely logical point of view, *who we are* shouldn't have anything to do with the worthiness of *what we say*. After all, the silliest or meanest person in the world could say that ''two plus two equals four,'' but that wouldn't make the statement wrong. However, it's a mistake to conclude that who we are has nothing to do with how an audience reacts to the things we say.

THIS IS NOT EXACTLY THE BEST WAY TO WIN OTHERS TO YOUR POINT OF VIEW.

COMMUNICATION MYTH #7

COMMUNICATION MYTH #7: A logical, perfect argument will always persuade an audience.

AUDIENCE PERCEPTIONS

This is a myth and not fact for two reasons. First, most people have never been trained in formal logic and reasoning. Most of us never get beyond the surface of this specialized area of study. That is not as important as the second reason why a logical, perfect argument won't always persuade an audience:

Formal logic, with all its rules and principles, does not describe the way people think and decide in everyday situations!

Humans use ''all of themselves'' when they think and decide about matters—not just their abilities to reason ''logically.'' They also use their feelings, their likes and dislikes, their loyalties, their values, and even their sense of humor. All of these factors contribute in some combination to their decisions.

And you, the person communicating with your audience, become the focal point of all these factors. In short, *who you are* can speak just as loudly as *what you have to say!*

Your audience will perceive who you are from your communication in six specific areas:

1. Your expertise in the subject area being discussed.

2. Your personal commitment to the subject.

3. Your personal commitment to the audience.

4. Your character as a generally honest and trustworthy person.

5. Your personal dynamism and energy.

6. The persons, agencies, or institutions you represent.

AUDIENCE PERCEPTIONS

In any of the six areas listed on page 47, an unfavorable perception of you by your audience will influence its decision about your ideas.

For example: when candidates in an election try to win your vote, each of the six factors can influence or decide your choice.

Is the candidate:

☐ Experienced in the issues and problems associated with this office?

☐ Sincerely committed to doing the best job he or she can in office?

☐ Interested in OUR needs and wants?

☐ Trustworthy?

☐ A dynamic, engaging person?

☐ Representing a political party (or interest groups) that we respect and support?

Naturally, each factor will have more or less importance for different people. For example, if you are most interested in taxes, you might weigh the candidates' positions on this issue more carefully than the question of which party they belong to. On the other hand, party loyalty may overrule any feelings you might have that the candidate isn't very exciting.

CONFLICTING BELIEFS, ATTITUDES, OR VALUES

This source of resistance relates to the point recently made, namely: humans bring ''all of themselves'' into their decision-making, not just their ability to reason ''logically.''

We base our decisions and actions, as best we can, upon three things:

BELIEFS—our conviction that certain things are true, or that certain statements are facts.

ATTITUDES—our judgments that particular things are good or bad, desireable or undesireable, and so on.

VALUES—the larger, more general patterns of attitudes that are consistent across many areas of our lives.

And our attitudes and values are rarely consistent with one another.

DO YOU UNDERSTAND YOUR OWN BELIEFS,
ATTITUDES & VALUES?

CASE PROBLEM:
BELIEFS, ATTITUDES, AND VALUES

Imagine that you are a supervisor for a company that makes precision engineering parts. One of your workers, Ann, notices that your company sells a component to the military for three dollars, and the same component to civilian purchasers for only one dollar. She reports the difference to you, and you explain that the difference in price is because the company is required to do additional quality and safety testing on the parts supplied to the government, but not on those supplied to civilian customers. You remind Ann that an investigation into the problem would cause delays that could cost the company the government contract, even if the company is not found to be at fault. Ann's decision about how to handle this situation will be the product of different beliefs, attitudes, and values:

Some of Ann's *beliefs* might include:

- She trusts you, her supervisor.

- She feels your company hasn't always obeyed the law in government contract work.

- She believes the information on the difference in prices is apparently reliable.

Some of Ann's *attitudes* might include:

- She likes her job.

- She prefers a good relationship with her supervisor.

- Keeping quiet about possible ''price fixing'' would be wrong.

Some of Ann's *values* might include:

- It is important to behave ethically when the trust of the public is involved.

- People should be loyal to their employer.

- People should be loyal to the people they work with.

Before we could predict how Ann would react to your request that she drop the issue, we would have to consider all three of these areas. Various attitudes, values, or beliefs will carry different weights in her choice, and other people in Ann's situation might weigh the factors differently than she would. Ann's problem is that she is UNDECIDED—that is, that the conflicting attitudes, values, and beliefs don't yet clearly point to a single course of action.

As we have just seen, conflicting beliefs, attitudes, or values lead to indecision. Another side to the problem is that sometimes people know the proper conclusion to draw, or the proper attitude to take, but they find it easier to rationalize away or minimize the issue itself.

***NEVER RELY ON THIS WHEN DEALING
WITH ATTITUDES, VALUES, OR BELIEFS***

COMMUNICATION MYTH #8

COMMUNICATION MYTH #8: Give people the "facts" and they will always believe as you do, or act as you'd like them to act.

Consider a familiar example: How many times a week do you read, see, or hear an appeal for some worthy charity? For most of us, the answer is "many times"—considering how overexposed we are to magazine ads, television spots, radio messages, mass mailings, billboards, telephone solicitations, etc.! For better or worse, we usually don't respond to most of the appeals for charitable donations. It isn't because we are selfish or uncharitable. And it's not because we don't know the "facts" about the good works these charities do! It is because, for whatever reason, we don't feel a strong enough impulse to act on our sympathies. Think about how many persuasive campaigns are based, at least in part, on the popular assumption that giving people "the facts" will cause them to behave or believe as we'd like. Some examples include:

Always using seat belts or shoulder belts when driving.

Avoiding dangers or tobacco, alcohol, or other chemical abuse.

Exercising the right to vote.

Yet, in all of the above cases, people who ignore the advice are usually aware of the "facts" supporting each issue. They don't find these facts motivating enough to change their behavior. In other words, they find other advice more compelling when it comes to their attitudes, beliefs, or values.

In the terms of Section II, such people are NEUTRAL. They understand what these persuasive messages want them to do, but don't feel sufficiently motivated by the messages. Perhaps they feel that the topic isn't that important to them, or that their actions wouldn't make any difference.

COMMUNICATION MYTH #9

COMMUNICATION MYTH #9: Facts are facts.

For many managers it is a "fact" that they represent the interests of their organization better than union officials who, in turn, find the superiority of their own outlook to be a matter of "fact," too. Be very wary of the word "facts"—it often means values, attitudes, or beliefs that we don't question, but that other people might!

The best rule of thumb is: facts are only facts when all sides agree to them—one side in a disagreement can't simply declare something to be a fact.

"TO SUPPORT MY POSITION, LET'S LOOK AT SOME FACTS."

A NOTE ABOUT "INFORMATION" AND "FACTS"

Many people mistakenly imagine that *all* differences of attitudes, values, beliefs, or actions are simply because "they" don't have access to the same "facts" that "we" have—yet that's not so! When our attempts to influence others aren't successful, not getting the "facts" across is only ONE possible reason for failure. Other reasons may be our credibility as a communicator, conflicting values, or apathy. Consider all of the factors that influence an audience before jumping to conclusions.

Also remember that "facts" themselves are very slippery, and what we call a "fact" another person may call a "headstrong opinion."

REVIEW: IDENTIFYING SOURCES OF RESISTANCE IN DIFFERENT SITUATIONS

Use the following cases to practice understanding the sources of resistance to persuasive communication. Compare your answers to those on the pages following this review.

COMMUNICATOR'S IMAGE

In each of the following situations, an individual is preparing to influence others through his or her communication. Check those aspects of the communicator's image that would seem likely to play an important part (for better or worse) in successfully influencing the audience.

CASE #1: After the breakdown of a particularly hostile bargaining session between the teachers and the board of a local school corporation, a retired superintendent from the district offers her services as a mediator to get negotiations started again. She has come to a meeting of the teachers to discuss reopening contract talks. This negotiator offers:

☐ Expertise

☐ Commitment to the subject

☐ Commitment to the audience

☐ Trustworthy character

☐ Personal dynamism and energy

☐ Institution represented

CASE #2: A homeowner answers his phone on a weeknight. The call is from a young woman who is offering customers the chance to purchase home repair products such as weatherproof siding. This salesperson offers:

☐ Expertise

☐ Commitment to the subject

☐ Commitment to the audience

☐ Trustworthy character

☐ Personal dynamism and energy

☐ Institution represented

CASE #3: Following the retirement of a much-liked office supervisor, the new supervisor holds a meeting to discuss some changes to be made in office procedures. Many of these changes stem from cut-backs forced on the office by top management. The new supervisor is young, not well-known, and not as socially outgoing as the former supervisor. This supervisor offers:

- ☐ Expertise
- ☐ Commitment to the subject
- ☐ Commitment to the audience
- ☐ Trustworthy character
- ☐ Personal dynamism and energy
- ☐ Institution represented

CONFLICTING ATTITUDES, VALUES AND BELIEFS

CASE #4: Jane is deciding whether to wear her seat belt while driving her car. What attitudes, values, and beliefs could influence her decision FOR or AGAINST wearing the seat belt?

_____

_____

_____

_____

APATHY OR SKEPTICISM

CASE #5: Suppose that you are a candidate for local office. In your campaign speeches, ads, and pamphlets, you stress three themes: reducing local property taxes; encouraging businesses to redevelop the town's downtown area; and improving the quality of the local schools. You have engagements to speak to two groups today: the local parent-teachers organization and a local historical society. Circle what might be the initial interest level of each group on the issues.

	Interest Level	
Issues	**Parent-Teachers**	**Historical Society**
1. Reducing local property taxes	high low	high low
2. Encouraging downtown redevelopment	high low	high low
3. Improving quality of schools	high low	high low

AUTHOR RESPONSE TO CASES

Your answers may vary from those below, that's o.k.. What is important is that your answers reflect the principles described earlier in this Section.

CASE #1

☑ Expertise

☑ Commitment to the subject

This retired superintendent-turned-mediator has two positive credibility factors. As a former superintendent she will probably be perceived as having expertise with the issues involved in the negotiation. Her personal commitment to the subject is indicated by the offer to ''come out of retirement'' for such a challenging task.

As a mediator she needn't (and shouldn't) portray herself as committed to the teachers. Likewise, it is important that she not be perceived as being ''for'' the administration—an especially important issue, since she was formerly an administrator herself.

One other important aspect of her image is that, as a volunteer mediator, she doesn't represent any institution or agency, therefore she doesn't have the authority to impose or enforce any resolution—and both sides will be aware of this.

CASE #2

☑ Expertise

☑ Commitment to the subject

☑ Personal dynamism and energy

☑ Institution represented

Telephone solicitors face a difficult persuasive task. With a high refusal rate they need a high volume of customer calls to guarantee a high sales volume. Part of the reason for refusals has to do with the image of the communicator himself or herself.

Telephone solicitors are usually perceived as having a low commitment to the customer—since ''blind'' phone calls are pretty impersonal. A poorly trained caller aggravates the problem even more: a poor or unprepared delivery (where the voice is the only medium!) conveys an image of low dynamism and energy; and any unfamiliarity with the product (as often happens with telephone solicitors) fairly shouts ''little commitment to the topic!''

A poised, polite, energetic, well-prepared caller from a reputable firm will have the most credibility in such a situation.

CASE# 3

If you didn't check any characteristics you were right. This supervisor doesn't seem to have any characteristics that will help to establish a positive image with his department.

A personal relationship with an audience often helps a communicator's credibility. Yet this supervisor hasn't been in this department long, has replaced a popular supervisor, and has a very different interpersonal style from the former supervisor. The basis for an ongoing sense of trust between the supervisor and the department is not in place yet.

This problem may be aggravated by another factor in the description: he is bringing bad news to the office (changes related to cutbacks). In addition, although there's nothing specific in the description, if the new supervisor is unusually young, this may hamper his credibility by calling into question his experience and competence.

CASE #4

Jane's potentially life-saving choice will be influenced by many factors that Jane believes, values, and prefers. Such factors will probably include:

> The statistics she's heard about lives saved by using seat belts.
> The extent to which she believes those statistics about seat belts.
> The extent to which she believes those statistics apply to her.
> The importance of her trip, and of getting there on time.
> The likelihood of having an accident while driving.
> Her knowledge of the law in her state requiring seat belt use.
> The importance she places upon obeying the law.
> How she feels about who is travelling with her.
> Whether her fellow passengers use their seatbelts.

If Jane is like most of us, when she gets in her car she weighs all these factors together in a split second and without realizing it she uses them to make her decision. And as we all know, it's not uncommon for sensible people to choose comfort and convenience instead of putting on their seat belts, even though they believe it's legal and safer to use them! Perhaps they think that the seat belt laws are silly, or that "accidents won't happen to them"—but such decisions, like most we all make, involve ALL of our related beliefs, attitudes, and values, sifted and weighed together.

AUTHOR RESPONSE TO CASES
(Continued)

CASE #5

	Interest Level	
Issues	**Parent-Teachers**	**Historical Society**
1. Reducing local property taxes	(high) low	high ? low
2. Encouraging downtown redevelopment	high (low)	(high) low
3. Improving quality of schools	(high) low	high ? low

It seems likely that the parent-teacher group would be very interested in the education issue. And, if the property tax issue affects the amount of public funds available for the school, that group would be interested in that issue as well. In the description, no reason is given to suggest that this audience is interested in the downtown renovation issue. As we discussed in Section II, many audiences are formed because of the common interests they share, and knowing how the audience was formed will tell you about their interests, attitudes, and expectations.

It may be less easy to guess what will most strongly motivate the local historical society. Perhaps the downtown renovation, because it may have implications for historic landmarks. As taxpayers and parents, they may also have an interest in property tax and education issues, as well, although that interest does not relate to their membership in the historical society. The moral, once again, comes from Section II: if you don't have the information you want and need about your audience, DO YOUR HOMEWORK! Try and find information about the audience before you face it, so you can form your best strategy.

WHAT'S NEXT?

We've looked at some of the reasons why the people we try to influence may be UNFRIENDLY, or NEUTRAL, or UNDECIDED. In Section IV, we'll look at communication strategies specifically designed to overcome sources of resistance.

SECTION IV: OVERCOMING RESISTANCE TO PERSUASION

"MISS JONES, THESE FRIENDLY FOLKS WANT TO LEARN MORE ABOUT OUR NO REFUND POLICY. COULD YOU PLEASE HELP THEM?"

In this Section you will examine strategies for overcoming the specific sources of resistance when you are communicating with others. Specific strategies can be used to overcome the three problem areas discussed in Section III—image problems; conflicting values, attitudes, or beliefs; or apathy or skepticism.

OVERCOMING IMAGE PROBLEMS

Your credibility—your image as a competent, honest, dynamic communicator who is concerned about the audience's needs and values as much as his or her own—is your most important asset as a communicator. Look for opportunities to use the following techniques to enhance your credibility:

- Be *prepared* to communicate with your audience. Know your purpose, and know your audience. Don't improvise as you go!

- Make sure that the audience *knows* about your credentials, expertise, education, etc., if these are going to influence how they perceive you and your message.

- Especially if it is an occasion calling for *formal* speaking or writing, take great care with the appearance of your message. Written messages should be clear, proofread, and neat. Oral presentations should be rehearsed, clear, and (as appropriate) use supplemental audio or visual materials that are appropriate, professional-looking, and understandable.

- Communicate in a way that is *enthusiastic* and energetic. In writing, use language that is active and forceful. In speaking, be aware that not just your words, but your voice and actions contribute to your credibility. Make sure that your presentation—written or oral—is smooth, polished, and confident.

- *Don't assume* that your audience knows that you understand and respect their point of view—show them! Work with what's familiar to them when you refer to examples, mention names, use technical terms, or explain reasons.

- Use the endorsement or support of persons your audience perceives to have high credibility to enhance your own image. If you're not perceived as an expert yourself, show that you have studied the experts. If you're not well-known to the audience, show that you represent persons who are well-known to them.

OVERCOMING CONFLICTING AUDIENCE ATTITUDES, VALUES, OR BELIEFS

The problem of conflicting attitudes or beliefs is a common one when influencing others. It is so complex that the strategies listed below may not be sufficient, but they should help. Look for opportunities to use the following techniques. Check those you expect to use:

- When it can be done tactfully, draw attention to the conflict itself. We all like to feel that we're thinking and acting in consistent ways. Educating an audience about conflict between their actions and their attitudes, values, and beliefs is a powerful motivator. Audiences can be motivated to change their thoughts or actions when these items are clearly shown to be in conflict.

- If the conflict is only an apparent one (that is, there is no real contradiction in attitudes, beliefs, or values to prevent the audience from supporting you) show them. This situation may apply especially to when the audience is unfamiliar or uninformed.

- If the conflict can't be resolved, can it be downplayed? Look for ways to minimize the importance of the conflict between different attitudes, beliefs, and values.

- Look for authority figures to resolve the conflict. Are there respected individuals who support your position? Are there people in the same situation whose story can help the audience to change their position?

- In some cases, dwelling on the conflict may cause an audience to delay or avoid a decision rather than resolve the conflict. This is particularly true when the audience feels no action or decision needs resolution. In these cases, your challenge is to stress the urgency of the situation to act clearly and/or quickly.

OVERCOMING APATHY OR SKEPTICISM

Remember that responses to our persuasive appeals are not just based on logical reasoning. Peoples' feelings, wants, and preferences also contribute to the decision-making process. When an audience simply doesn't seem motivated enough to give their support to your ideas, requests, or plans, you have to devise ways of creating that motivation! Look for opportunities to use the following techniques:

Be Positive!

Where possible, motivate by appealing to positive emotions—such as hope, ambition, joy, gratitude, love, pride—rather than negative ones. There are two reasons for this:

- First, negative emotions—such as hate, envy, or fear—are very difficult to get out of the atmosphere once they've been let loose. You are familiar with cases in which ''negative advertising'' for a candidate, a cause, or a product has ''boomeranged'' by stirring a negative response from the audience directed toward the source of the message.

- Second, while it's difficult to imagine a message that created too much hope, or too much gratitude, it's not hard to imagine creating so much fear or unhappiness in an audience that they no longer feel able to respond.

While positive motivations have no real upper threshold, negative emotions do—pushing them too far causes them to lose their motivational value.

OVERCOMING APATHY OR SKEPTICISM (Continued)

BE POSITIVE!

Think about the positive emotions you want to create and what causes them. What causes joy, gratitude, or hope? Then SHOW your audience, as clearly and vividly as you can, how these feelings are involved in the ideas you are communicating.

Think about what these positive emotions *look* and *feel* like. How do people look and act when they're excited, or optimistic, and so on? Then *show* your audience these images, as clearly and vividly as you can, by describing or introducing other people who are motivated, *and by showing these characteristics in yourself*! Nothing can undermine your attempts to influence others like looking disinterested when you're talking about optimism, looking bored when you're talking about hope, or looking irritated when talking about gratitude. Show your audience positive emotions, and that you understand them, in your own words and actions and in the words and actions of others! ''Like kindles like''—enthusiasm kindles enthusiasm.

REVIEW: SELECTING PERSUASIVE STRATEGIES— THREE CASES

In each of the following cases, assume that you are facing the audience described, in an attempt to persuade them to take a particular course of action, or to adopt a particular attitude. In each case, answer two questions:

1. What is the *source* of the resistance you face in that audience? (Note that there may be more than one source in a particular audience!)

2. What particular *strategies* are most appropriate to overcome the source(s) of resistance in this audience?

Compare your answers with those of the author on page 67.

CASE #1: You are the representative for the local Red Cross. You have come to the employee meeting of a local department store to ask the workers to donate blood in the annual blood drive. Turnout from this store has always been somewhat low. It is the holiday season when the local hospital's need for blood is highest.

Source of Resistance: _____

Strategies: _____

_____

_____

_____

_____

_____

_____

_____

SELECTING PERSUASIVE STRATEGIES—THREE CASES (Continued)

CASE #2: You are the head of the purchasing department at your company. Your vice-president has called you to a meeting to discuss your proposal that various office heads no longer be able to sign their own requisitions. You have carefully documented the additional expense that the current purchasing system has caused the company—chiefly because different offices are duplicating purchases, making unnecessary purchases, and hiring outside services that are available (with patience) in-house. The vice president was instrumental in getting the current system approved four years ago. You and the vice president are not close friends, but have known one another and gotten along well for ten years.

Source of Resistance: _____

Strategies: _____

_____

_____

_____

_____

_____

_____

_____

SELECTING PURSUASIVE STRATEGIES—THREE CASES (Continued)

CASE #3: Now think about some situation you're going to be facing—at work, at school, in some group or organization you belong to—where you'd like to influence your audience to support (or stop hindering) your ideas or plans. Ask yourself the very same questions:

Source of Resistance: _____

Strategies: _____

_____

_____

_____

_____

_____

_____

_____

_____

AUTHOR RESPONSE TO SELECTING PERSUASIVE STRATEGIES

> **CASE #1:**   This is a complex case. Your audience has aspects of three types of audiences: NEUTRAL, UNDECIDED, and UNFRIENDLY: Like NEUTRAL audiences, they may understand the importance of donating blood, but fail to see how it affects them personally. Like UNDECIDED audiences, they may appreciate the importance of donating blood, but be afraid of the procedure. They may be disturbed by the health risk posed by blood-transmitted diseases, even though donation procedures are protected against such risk. Like UNFRIENDLY audiences, they may simply not want to donate blood.

STRATEGIES

The choice of strategies should reflect this complexity—no single approach is ''correct'', but some seem best to take into account the likely sources of resistance.

Sound strategy would advise you to avoid negative aspects of blood donation (i.e.—fear of needles, or fainting). For those who have never experienced it, needles can be vivid negative images—and don't need to be made even more dramatic by talking about them! Instead, work on the positive motivators—helping others, giving life, etc.. Many people don't think about donating blood because they aren't directly familiar with how it helps others. Help your audience imagine the good they'll be doing by relating vivid stories of real people in situations they can recognize and identify with.

Although there is no evidence that you would suffer any image problem in this situation, you might want to consider getting the top people in your organization to support you visibly—through endorsements, or even better, being the first to donate? Can you cultivate your relationship with your audience throughout the year, perhaps by sharing ''success stories'' or participating in programs that they support? This is an effective strategy which avoids being perceived as being around only when you ''want something.''

AUTHOR RESPONSES (Continued)

CASE #2:   This case is also complex. To the extent that your vice president may not have a full, accurate report of the additional costs of the present systems, she may simply be UNINFORMED. Here, your careful study and your generally good relationship with the vice president will work to your advantage. But, to the extent that the vice president feels a sense of pride or responsibility for the present system and might take a negative criticism of it as reflecting badly on herself, it would be more appropriate to regard the audience as at least slightly UNFRIENDLY. In this case, your lower status (compared to her) could work against you by making you appear insubordinate or disrespectful.

The fundamental conflict for your vice president is likely to take this form: On the one hand is the importance of good business practices and economy, plus the carefully documented evidence you have produced. On the other hand is the time and expense involved in changing the purchasing system as you suggest, plus the possibility of losing face because the old system isn't working.

STRATEGIES

Drawing attention to this conflict is probably not a good strategy, since it would risk forcing the vice president to confront something potentially unpleasant. It's probably safer to downplay the conflict, drawing no attention to the possibility of anyone losing face over this. At the same time, it would be appropriate to dwell on the positive motivations of accomplishment, initiative, and pride as reasons for implementing the new system. Make the advantages of the new system as easy to imagine as possible, stressing the savings under the system you propose (and any other advantages of it that would be relevant), stressing its value to the company's goals, and so on.

CASE #3: This is the real test—can you apply the principles of communication described in this book to solve your communication problems and meet your communication needs in dealing with others?

STRATEGIES

Remember to follow the guidelines from the earlier sections of this book!

FIRST, specify clearly your purpose in communicating.

SECOND, find out as much as you can about the AUDIENCE you will be speaking or writing to, and determine where they fall among the various audience types outlined in Section II.

THIRD, choose specific STRATEGIES for the type of audience you will face, as described in Section II.

FOURTH, try to determine specific causes for the attitudes, beliefs, or values of your audience, as covered in Section III.

FINALLY, select additional STRATEGIES for dealing with the causes of resistance in your audience.

SECTION V: FINAL REVIEW

In this book you have worked through a systematic approach to successfully influencing others in our communication. That approach is based on several important principles: having clear goals as a communicator; thinking carefully about the people with whom you are communicating—their feelings, wants, needs, and knowledge; and selecting clear strategies designed to meet these goals in your communication.

NINE RESOLUTIONS FOR EFFECTIVE PERSUASION

A good way to review—and to appreciate the progress you've made in understanding effective communication—is to emphasize those principles that are designed to help you overcome the "communication myths". I therefore offer you the following resolutions for your own communication. Check those you agree to follow.

☐ 1. I *resolve* to give careful and serious thought to my audience, to the positions they hold and to the reasons they have come to hold these positions. I reject "Communication Myth #1"—the belief that all I need to know about an audience is whether they're "for me" or "against me."

☐ 2. I *resolve* that, in addition to communicating clearly, I will communicate in ways that respect the individual differences among persons and audiences. I reject "Communication Myth #2"—the belief that all I have to worry about in effective communication is having a clear message.

☐ 3. I *resolve* to remember that even the most supportive audiences may still be engaged persuasively, to maintain their motivation, reaffirm their dedication, or focus their energy and enthusiasm. I reject "Communication Myth #3"—the belief that only UNFRIENDLY audiences require persuasive communication.

☐ 4. I *resolve* to set realistic goals as a persuader, to remember that attitudes, values, or beliefs are not found overnight, and often cannot be changed by a single message. I accept that any persuasive influence I have is a measure not only of my efforts, but also the willingness of my audience to allow me access to their judgments and actions. I reject "Communication Myth #4"—the belief that persuasion must totally convert even UNFRIENDLY audiences to be considered successful.

☐ 5. I *resolve* to remember that people judge and act differently from me for many reasons, and to accept that inadequate information is one possible reason that those around me may hold different attitudes. I reject "Communication Myth #5"—the belief that "persuading" and "informing" are two different kinds of communication.

NINE RESOLUTIONS (Continued)

☐ 6. I *resolve* to remember that people use the information I give them differently in different situations, and that no single type of evidence or proof will always persuade, regardless of audience or subject. I *reject* ''Communication Myth #6''—the belief that the best way to influence people is always with statistics.

☐ 7. I *resolve* to accept that my audience is complex and responds in complicated ways to things they hear and read—just as I do. I accept that all of us respond with ''all parts of ourselves'' to the communication around us—not only with reason, but with our feelings, tastes, attitudes, and values. I *reject* ''Communication Myth #7''—the belief that a logically perfect presentation will always persuade an audience.

☐ 8. I *resolve* to accept that ''facts'' are only one part of the basis upon which people think, feel, and act. I *reject* ''Communication Myth #8''—the belief that if people know the ''facts'' they will always believe as I do, or act as I'd like them to act.

☐ 9. I *resolve* to accept the right of others to interpret events around them in their own way, just as I reserve that right for myself. I accept the right of others to question or challenge my claims, even if those claims seem, for me to be beyond doubt. I *reject* ''Communication Myth #9''—the belief that ''facts'' are ''facts.''

RESOLVE NOT TO LET THIS HAPPEN TO YOU!

$$\boxed{\textbf{NOTES}}$$

$$\boxed{\begin{array}{c}\text{FOR OTHER FIFTY-MINUTE SELF-STUDY BOOKS}\\\text{SEE ORDER FORM AT THE BACK OF THE BOOK.}\end{array}}$$

NOTES

FOR OTHER FIFTY-MINUTE SELF-STUDY BOOKS
SEE ORDER FORM AT THE BACK OF THE BOOK.

NOTES

FOR OTHER FIFTY-MINUTE SELF-STUDY BOOKS
SEE ORDER FORM AT THE BACK OF THE BOOK.

NOTES

FOR OTHER FIFTY-MINUTE SELF-STUDY BOOKS
SEE ORDER FORM AT THE BACK OF THE BOOK.

$$\boxed{\textbf{NOTES}}$$

FOR OTHER FIFTY-MINUTE SELF-STUDY BOOKS
SEE ORDER FORM AT THE BACK OF THE BOOK.

ABOUT THE FIFTY-MINUTE SERIES

''Every so often an idea emerges that is so simple and appealing, people wonder why it didn't come along sooner. The Fifty-Minute series is just such an idea. Excellent!''

Mahaliah Levine, Vice President for
Training and Development
Dean Witter Reynolds, Inc.

WHAT IS A FIFTY-MINUTE BOOK?

—Fifty-Minute books are brief, soft-covered, ''self-study'' titles covering a wide variety of topics pertaining to business and self-improvement. They are reasonably priced, ideal for formal training, excellent for self-study and perfect for remote location training.

''A Fifty-Minute book gives the reader fundamentals that can be applied on the job, even before attending a formal class''

Lynn Baker, Manager of Training
Fleming Corporation

WHY ARE FIFTY-MINUTE BOOKS UNIQUE?

—Because of their format. Designed to be ''read with a pencil,'' the basics of a subject can be quickly grasped and applied through a series of hands-on activities, exercises and cases.

''Fifty-Minute books are the best new publishing idea in years. They are clear, practical, concise and affordable—perfect for today's world.''

Leo Hauser, Past President
ASTD

HOW MANY FIFTY-MINUTE BOOKS ARE THERE?

—Those listed on the following pages at this time. Additional titles are always in development. For more information write to **Crisp Publications, Inc.,** **95 First Street, Los Altos, CA 94022.**

THE FIFTY-MINUTE SERIES

Quantity	Title	Code #	Price	Amount
	MANAGEMENT TRAINING			
	Successful Negotiation	09-2	$7.95	
	Personal Performance Contracts	12-2	$7.95	
	Team Building	16-5	$7.95	
	Effective Meeting Skills	33-5	$7.95	
	An Honest Day's Work	39-4	$7.95	
	Managing Disagreement Constructively	41-6	$7.95	
	Training Managers To Train	43-2	$7.95	
	The Fifty-Minute Supervisor	58-0	$7.95	
	Leadership Skills For Women	62-9	$7.95	
	Systematic Problem Solving & Decision Making	63-7	$7.95	
	Coaching & Counseling	68-8	$7.95	
	Ethics in Business	69-6	$7.95	
	Understanding Organizational Change	71-8	$7.95	
	Project Management	75-0	$7.95	
	Managing Organizational Change	80-7	$7.95	
	Working Together	85-8	$7.95	
	Financial Planning With Employee Benefits	90-4	$7.95	
	PERSONNEL TRAINING & HUMAN RESOURCE MANAGEMENT			
	Effective Performance Appraisals	11-4	$7.95	
	Quality Interviewing	13-0	$7.95	
	Personal Counseling	14-9	$7.95	
	Job Performance and Chemical Dependency	27-0	$7.95	
	New Employee Orientation	46-7	$7.95	
	Professional Excellence for Secretaries	52-1	$7.95	
	Guide To Affirmative Action	54-8	$7.95	
	Writing A Human Resource Manual	70-X	$7.95	
	COMMUNICATIONS			
	Effective Presentation Skills	24-6	$7.95	
	Better Business Writing	25-4	$7.95	
	The Business of Listening	34-3	$7.95	
	Writing Fitness	35-1	$7.95	
	The Art of Communicating	45-9	$7.95	
	Technical Presentation Skills	55-6	$7.95	
	Making Humor Work	61-0	$7.95	
	Visual Aids in Business	77-7	$7.95	
	Speedreading in Business	78-5	$7.95	
	Influencing Others: A Practical Guide	84-X	$7.95	
	SELF-MANAGEMENT			
	Balancing Home And Career	10-6	$7.95	
	Mental Fitness: A Guide to Emotional Health	15-7	$7.95	
	Personal Financial Fitness	20-3	$7.95	
	Attitude: Your Most Priceless Possession	21-1	$7.95	
	Personal Time Management	22-X	$7.95	

(Continued on next page)

THE FIFTY-MINUTE SERIES

Quantity	Title	Code #	Price	Amount
	SELF-MANAGEMENT (CONTINUED)			
	Preventing Job Burnout	23-8	$7.95	
	Successful Self-Management	26-2	$7.95	
	Developing Positive Assertiveness	38-6	$7.95	
	Time Management And The Telephone	53-X	$7.95	
	Memory Skills In Business	56-4	$7.95	
	Developing Self-Esteem	66-1	$7.95	
	Creativity In Business	67-X	$7.95	
	Managing Personal Change	74-2	$7.95	
	Winning At Human Relations	86-6	$7.95	
	Stop Procrastinating	88-2	$7.95	
	SALES TRAINING/QUALITY CUSTOMER SERVICE			
	Sales Training Basics	02-5	$7.95	
	Restaurant Server's Guide	08-4	$7.95	
	Quality Customer Service	17-3	$7.95	
	Telephone Courtesy And Customer Service	18-1	$7.95	
	Professional Selling	42-4	$7.95	
	Customer Satisfaction	57-2	$7.95	
	Telemarketing Basics	60-2	$7.95	
	Calming Upset Customers	65-3	$7.95	
	Quality At Work	72-6	$7.95	
	Managing A Quality Service Organization	83-1	$7.95	
	ENTREPRENEURSHIP			
	Marketing Your Consulting Or Professional Services	40-8	$7.95	
	Starting Your Small Business	44-0	$7.95	
	Publicity Power	82-3	$7.95	
	CAREER GUIDANCE & STUDY SKILLS			
	Study Skills Strategies	05-X	$7.95	
	Career Discovery	07-6	$7.95	
	Plan B: Protecting Your Career From The Winds of Change	48-3	$7.95	
	I Got The Job!	59-9	$7.95	
	OTHER CRISP INC. BOOKS			
	Comfort Zones: A Practical Guide For Retirement Planning	00-9	$13.95	
	Stepping Up To Supervisor	11-8	$13.95	
	The Unfinished Business Of Living: Helping Aging Parents	19-X	$12.95	
	Managing Performance	23-7	$18.95	
	Be True To Your Future: A Guide to Life Planning	47-5	$13.95	
	Up Your Productivity	49-1	$10.95	
	How To Succeed In A Man's World	79-3	$7.95	
	Practical Time Management	275-4	$13.95	
	Copyediting: A Practical Guide	51-3	$18.95	

THE FIFTY-MINUTE SERIES
(Continued)

☐ Send volume discount information.

☐ Please send me a catalog.

	Amount
Total (from other side)	
Shipping ($1.50 first book, $.50 per title thereafter)	
California Residents add 7% tax	
Total	

Ship to: _____

_____

_____

_____

Phone number: _____

Bill to: _____

_____

_____

_____

P.O. # _____

All orders except those with a P.O.# must be prepaid.
For more information Call (415) 949-4888 or FAX (415) 949-1610.

BUSINESS REPLY
FIRST CLASS   PERMIT NO. 884   LOS ALTOS, CA

POSTAGE WILL BE PAID BY ADDRESSEE

Crisp Publications, Inc.
95 First Street
Los Altos, CA 94022

NO POSTAGE
NECESSARY
IF MAILED
IN THE
UNITED STATES